CONTENTS

CONTENTS

INTRODUCTION

INTRODUCTION

A ferry crosses the water at the busy port of Shanghai near the mouth of the Yangtze. The river travels nearly 4,000 miles (6,400 km), from its source in the mountains of western China to the East China Sea.

YANGTZE FACTS

- Length: 3,900 miles (6,275 km)
- Drainage basin: 700,000 square miles
  (1,813,000 square kilometers)
- Main cities: Shanghai, Chongqing, Wuhan, Nanjing
- Major tributaries: Min River, Gan River, Yuan River, and
  Xiang River (700 tributaries total)

The Long River

The Yangtze River flows through the heart of China. From its **source** in the mountains of western China, the river flows eastward across the plains until it reaches the East China Sea. The Yangtze River stretches for 3,900 miles (6,275 kilometers). It is the third longest river in the world, after the Nile River in Africa and the Amazon River in South America. The Chinese call the Yangtze Chang Jiang, which means "Long River."

Settlements and temples dating back 2,000 years can be found along the banks of the Yangtze, where many Chinese legends have been set. Just beyond the city of Chongqing, the river passes through the famous Three **Gorges**, a series of steep gorges surrounded by towering mountains. The gorges have been celebrated in Chinese art and poetry, and today they are among the most visited tourist attractions in China.

Please visit our web site at: www.worldalmanaclibrary.com
For a free color catalog describing World Almanac® Library's list of high-quality
books and multimedia programs, call 1-800-848-2928 (USA) or 1-800-387-3178 (Canada).
World Almanac® Library's fax: (414) 332-3567.

Library of Congress Cataloging-in-Publication Data

Waterlow, Julia.
  The Yangtze / Julia Waterlow.
     p. cm. — (Great rivers of the world)
  Includes bibliographical references and index.
  Contents: The course of the Yangtze — The Yangtze in history — Cities and settlements —
Economic activity — Animals and plants — Environmental issues — Leisure and recreation —
The future.
  ISBN 0-8368-5447-0 (lib. bdg.)
  ISBN 0-8368-5454-3 (softcover)
  1. Yangtze River (China)—Juvenile literature. [1. Yangtze River (China).] I. Title.
II. Series.
  DS793.Y3W39   2003
  951'.2—dc21   2002033134

First published in 2003 by
World Almanac® Library
330 West Olive Street, Suite 100
Milwaukee, WI 53212 USA

Copyright © 2003 by World Almanac® Library.

Developed by Monkey Puzzle Media
Editor: Jane Bingham
Designer: Tim Mayer
Picture researcher: Lynda Lines
World Almanac® Library editor: Jim Mezzanotte
World Almanac® Library art direction: Tammy Gruenewald

Picture acknowledgements
AKG London, 17 (Visioars); Alamy, 5 (View Stock China), 7 (Robert Harding), 9 (View Stock China), 30 (P. Oxford), 31 (J. Bower);
Corbis, front cover (Dena Conger), 38 (Tom Nebbia), 41 (Keren Su); Mark Henley, 20, 29, 43; Impact, 12 (Alain Le Garsmeur),
19 (Mark Henley), 21 (Mark Henley), 27 (Mark Henley), 36 (Mark Henley), 39 (Mark Henley), 42 (Mark Henley), 44 (Mark Henley),
45 (Robert Hind); Mary Evans Picture Library, 13, 14, 15; Robert Harding Picture Library, 16 (Gavin Hellier), 26 (Paolo Koch);
Still Pictures, 1 (Ingrid Moorjohn), 4 (Hartmut Schwarzbach), 22 (Thomas Kelly), 23 (Peter Arnold), 24 (Julio Etchart), 25 (Ingrid
Moorjohn), 28 (Hartmut Schwarzbach), 32 (Mark Carwardine), 33 (Tao Pu), 35 (Hartmut Schwarzbach); Travel Ink 11 (Derek Allan).
Map artwork by Peter Bull.

Printed in the United States of America

1 2 3 4 5 6 7 8 9 07 06 05 04 03

Great
Rivers
of the World

THE YANGTZE

Julia Waterlow

WORLD ALMANAC® LIBRARY

A Useful River

For centuries, the Yangtze was the main transportation route from China's coast to its central region. Large boats can travel for about 1,500 miles (2,400 km) along the river, and some of China's largest cities lie along its banks. Today, these cities are linked by railway, road, and air, but they are still important ports for traffic on the river.

The Yangtze River is the main source of water for the fertile farming land in the eastern lowlands of China. About a quarter of China's farmland lies within the Yangtze **basin**. This basin is the area drained by the Yangtze and the rivers that flow into it, which are known as its **tributaries**. The Yangtze is also used to supply electricity to China's huge and growing population. One of the world's largest **hydroelectric** dams is being built on the river.

The Yangtze River is full of activity for much of its length, but it also has peaceful stretches. For hundreds of years, Chinese poets have written about the Yangtze, while Chinese artists have painted its scenery — especially the section of the river known as the Three Gorges, which is shown below.

> **❝ The Yangtze River is a highway, workplace, backyard, well, and drain. ❞**
> Valerie Waggot, *China Now* (1993)

Chapter 1

THE COURSE OF THE YANGTZE

THE COURSE OF THE YANGTZE

The Roof of the World

The source of the Yangtze is a stream near Mount Geladandong, a 21,700-foot (6,600-meter) mountain in western China. Mount Geladandong is located on a high, rocky area of land called the Tibetan **Plateau**.

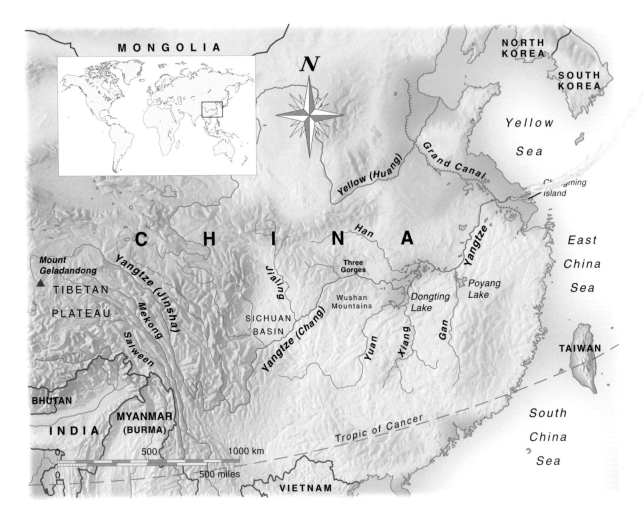

This map shows the course of the Yangtze River and its main tributaries.

This plateau is sometimes known as "the roof of the world." It has an elevation of over 10,000 feet (3,050 m) and is cold and windswept for most of the year.

The highest mountains on the Tibetan Plateau are covered with snow and ice. When some of this snow and ice melts, water gathers on the plateau and forms streams, lakes, and marshes. The Yangtze begins as one of these small wandering streams. It flows east, gathering more water from other streams, and it gradually grows into a river.

Rushing Water

As it leaves the Tibetan Plateau, the Yangtze changes dramatically. It becomes a fast-flowing torrent of water that plunges through gorges and ravines. In places, the river valley is 1.5 miles (2.4 km) deep, and it is so steep there is barely room for a path beside the river. Long stretches of the river consist of rapids. The Chinese call this dramatic stretch of the Yangtze the Jinsha, or "Golden Sand," River. Flowing south, the river runs parallel to two other great Asian rivers, the Mekong and the Salween. At some points, all three rivers flow in gorges that are less than 40 miles (64 km) apart.

Millions of years ago, the river we call the Yangtze continued south for its entire length, flowing through present-day Vietnam to the ocean. Then a range of high mountains formed in southern China, blocking the river's course and changing its direction. The modern Yangtze turns sharply north at the village of Shigu and then twists through steep valleys.

The Yangtze River cuts through mountains on the edge of the Tibetan Plateau, its waters rushing through canyons such as the one pictured above, known as Tiger Leaping Gorge. Travel is difficult in this region, and few people live there.

THE TIBETAN PLATEAU

The Tibetan Plateau is a vast area of high land to the north of the Himalayas mountain system. About 50 million years ago, two giant sections of Earth's crust, called plates, began grinding against each other. One plate gradually thrust under the other plate, pushing it upward. The Tibetan Plateau is believed to have formed about 13 million years ago, with more recent, violent movements of Earth forming the Himalayas.

The Sichuan Basin

Beyond the mountains of western China, the Yangtze River flows through a region of flatter land known as the Sichuan basin, where it becomes wider and slower-moving.

This region was originally part of a huge sea covering southeast Asia, but about 50 million years ago, powerful movements in Earth's crust began creating a range of mountains that cut off the area from the ocean. Rivers from mountains surrounding the area ran down into it and formed a huge lake. Over millions of years, water from the lake eventually carved a route through the Wushan Mountains to the east. The lake gradually drained away, leaving the fertile land of the Sichuan basin.

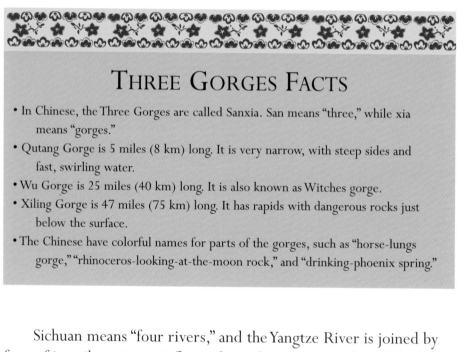

THREE GORGES FACTS

• In Chinese, the Three Gorges are called Sanxia. San means "three," while xia means "gorges."
• Qutang Gorge is 5 miles (8 km) long. It is very narrow, with steep sides and fast, swirling water.
• Wu Gorge is 25 miles (40 km) long. It is also known as Witches gorge.
• Xiling Gorge is 47 miles (75 km) long. It has rapids with dangerous rocks just below the surface.
• The Chinese have colorful names for parts of the gorges, such as "horse-lungs gorge," "rhinoceros-looking-at-the-moon rock," and "drinking-phoenix spring."

Sichuan means "four rivers," and the Yangtze River is joined by four of its tributaries as it flows along the southern edge of the basin. These tributaries add enormous amounts of water to the Yangtze, which swells dramatically. The rivers that cross the Sichuan basin cut through low hills of soft red sandstone, and the basin is sometimes called the "red basin" because of this sandstone. The basin's rich soil is very good for farming.

Mountain Gorges

Continuing eastward, the waters of the Yangtze cut through the Wushan Mountains, where the river narrows and surges through the Three Gorges. At one point, the river is only 350 feet (105 m) wide. The Chinese consider the Three Gorges to be the most beautiful stretch of the Yangtze. The gorges are formed mostly from limestone and have very steep sides with pinnacles of rock jutting out. Along this stretch, the river is extremely dangerous for boats. During winter, when the water level is low, boats can be caught on underwater rocks, and during the summer, when the river is full, the water surges through the gorges at an amazing speed. Each gorge has its own history, legends, and dangers.

About halfway along its course, the Yangtze flows through a route carved in the Wushan Mountains. This famous stretch of the river, known as the Three Gorges, receives millions of tourists every year.

Toward the East China Sea

Beyond the Three Gorges, the Yangtze becomes wider and flows more slowly. This stretch of the river is known as the lower Yangtze valley. For about 1,200 miles (1,930 km), until it reaches the ocean, the Yangtze **meanders** across a level, swampy plain. Several large tributaries join the Yangtze on this plain, which is crisscrossed by canals and waterways and studded with lakes. Two of these lakes, Poyang and Dongting, are the largest freshwater lakes in China.

From the city of Nanjing eastward to the coast, the Yangtze is almost at sea level. This stretch of the river is tidal, which means its water level changes as ocean tides rise and fall. When the tide in the East China Sea is high, water is pushed upriver and the water level rises. Water levels in the river fall when the tide is low.

Just before reaching the ocean, the river splits into two channels. This region is called the the Yangtze **delta**. The channels are separated by the island of Chongming. The island consists of **sediment**, which is soil and rock from upriver that travels down the river and is deposited in stretches of slower-moving water. The mouth of the river has marshes and sandbanks.

Flood Disasters

- 1931: **Dikes** fail all along the river and 150,000 people die.
- 1954: About 30,000 people die and millions become homeless.
- 1981: 1.5 million people along the Yangtze become homeless.
- 1988: About 3,000 people drown.
- 1991: 2,000 people die in floods along lower parts of the river.
- 1998: Over 3,000 people die. Cities along the Yangtze flood, and the damage costs China $38 billion.

Summer Floods

Water levels in the the Three Gorges section of the Yangtze River have been known to vary seasonally by as much as 200 feet (60 m). During the winter, when there is less rainfall, water levels are at their lowest. The river begins to rise in the spring, when melted snow runs down from the mountains. In the summer, the heavy **monsoon** rains arrive. Dongting and Poyang Lakes swell at this time, absorbing much of the monsoon rain and preventing too much water from flowing into the Yangtze. In years of exceptionally heavy rain, however, the Yangtze River floods, destroying farmland and sometimes towns and villages.

Over the last fifty years, flooding has been reduced through the construction of dikes along much of the river's lower course. The Chinese people have also built artificial lakes to hold excess floodwater. Despite these measures, flooding still occurs. As recently as 1998, parts of the city of Wuhan were several feet underwater.

A man wades past flooded houses. Every few years, the Yangtze River floods, and water spills out over farmland and into towns and cities. Heavy flooding along the Yangtze has occurred more than 200 times in the last 2,000 years.

Chapter 2

THE YANGTZE IN HISTORY

Early China

The earliest Chinese civilization was based in northern China, in the valley of China's other great river, the Yellow River. From about 1500 B.C., however, the Chinese began spreading south toward the Yangtze River. About 500 B.C., the middle stretches of the Yangtze were controlled by the kingdom of Chou. The Chou rulers had great armies and were constantly at war with other kingdoms. In 221 B.C., after Chou rule had collapsed, the neighboring kingdom of Ch'in unified China into one kingdom.

*Linggu Pagoda, in Nanjing, is part of a **Buddhist** temple complex. It was built about A.D. 1400 during the Ming dynasty, when Nanjing was the capital of China. After Mongols invaded from the north in the 1600s, China's capital was moved north to Beijing.*

Centers of Power

Chinese emperors, or rulers, were often part of a **dynasty** — a royal family that remained in power over several generations. By the time of the Sui dynasty (A.D. 589–618), the Yangtze basin was becoming the most important food-producing area of China. During this period, the Chinese built a long canal known as the Grand Canal. The canal stretched from the city of Hangzhou, just south of the Yangtze River in the lower Yangtze valley, to northern China. Barges traveling north on this canal shipped rice, salt, **tung oil**, silk, and tea.

As trade expanded in the lower Yangtze valley, cities in the region increased in size and power. Hangzhou developed into a major trading center. During the Sung dynasty (960–1279), it became the capital of China.

The Cutty Sark *was one of the most famous of the British "tea clippers," which were extremely fast sailing ships built during the 1800s to carry tea from China. At that time, China's tea was prized in both Europe and the United States.*

ALL THE TEA IN CHINA

- China has grown tea for at least 3,000 years. The Yangtze delta is one of the main tea-growing areas of China.
- Tea was first brought to Europe circa 1610. It gradually became a fashionable drink.
- By the early 1800s, China was supplying about 90 percent of the world's tea.

Between about A.D. 600 and 1280, during the T'ang and Sung dynasties, the city of Nanjing on the Yangtze rivaled Hangzhou as China's wealthiest city. During the Ming dynasty (1368–1644), the city became China's capital. Nanjing was a walled city with many palaces and magnificent buildings. It became famous for its civilized and cultured way of life and for the quality of the tea and silk that it produced.

Foreign Traders

During the **Middle Ages**, stories about China began reaching Europe through travelers such as Marco Polo. From the 1200s on, goods such as silk and spices were carried to Europe along overland trading routes in China, and by the 1600s European ships had reached China. Merchants came to trade in tea and silk — luxuries greatly prized in Europe. They were produced in the lower Yangtze valley, and the river became China's main shipping route. By the 1800s, British, U.S., and Russian ships arrived in China every May to buy tea. Towns on the Yangtze River, such as Wuhan, Nanjing, and Shanghai, developed into busy centers for foreign trade.

Travelers in China

The Chinese were suspicious of foreigners and only let them trade at certain ports in China. In 1842, however, Britain won a war against China that forced the Chinese to open up towns along the Yangtze River to foreigners and allow them to travel inland. Christian missionaries traveled deep into China and tried to convert the mainly Buddhist Chinese to Christianity. Explorers journeyed up the Yangtze and into the mountains of west Sichuan. Some explorers wrote books about their travels and took exotic Chinese plants home to their own countries.

Isabella Bird was a remarkable British explorer who came to China in 1896 at the age of sixty-four. She traveled far up the Yangtze and into the mountains, where no other foreigner had been before. On her return home, she wrote a book about her travels — The Yangtze River and Beyond.

War and Change

After the last Chinese dynasty, the Qing dynasty, was defeated in a revolution in 1911, more freedom existed in China. Many old traditions were abandoned, and wealthy, educated Chinese began to travel abroad. Beijing remained China's capital, but cities along the Yangtze, such as Shanghai, grew in importance because of foreign trade. Trade and shipping along the Yangtze river reached its peak in the 1920s and 1930s.

In 1938, as the Chinese fled from invading Japanese armies, the city of Chongqing on the Yangtze River briefly became China's capital. Millions of people came from eastern China to settle in Chongqing, which remained the capital of China until 1945.

MAO ZEDONG, COMMUNIST LEADER

Born in 1893 in Hunan province, just south of the Yangtze River, Mao Zedong was instrumental in introducing **communism** to China. He helped found the Communist Party in China and led the country for twenty-seven years. When Mao was seventy-three, he is said to have swum 9 miles (14.5 km) in the Yangtze River to prove he was still strong and healthy enough to run the country. He died in 1976.

During the first half of the twentieth century, most of China remained poor. The majority of Chinese were peasant farmers working land controlled by rich landlords. Many Chinese suffered from the Japanese invasion in the 1930s and a civil war in the 1940s. Natural disasters, such as floods on the Yangtze River, were made much worse because of the chaos.

This painting depicts Chinese fishermen being attacked by a Japanese submarine in 1937. When the Japanese invaded eastern China, many Chinese fled to Chongqing on the Yangtze River.

Communist China

When civil war ended in 1949, the Chinese Communist Party had won control of China. The communists took land from the landlords and gave it to millions of poor farmers. The government built houses, hospitals, schools, and factories, and it organized the construction of dikes, overflow lakes, dams, and **irrigation** channels along the Yangtze to control the river.

Culture and Religion

At various times during the Tang, Song, and Ming dynasties, from about A.D. 600 to 1600, many towns along the banks of the Yangtze river were religious and cultural centers. Chinese poets wrote about the joys and dangers of traveling along the river, as well as the beauty of the scenery. Painters drew bamboo, rocks, and water and showed swirling mists twisting around the peaks of mountains beside the river.

Religious Chinese found peaceful refuge in remote hills in the countryside surrounding the river. Many were **Taoists** who believed in living a simple, gentle life that did not disturb nature. Over the centuries, the teachings of the Taoists mingled with older Chinese beliefs in gods, spirits, and demons, and Taoism became a religion. Buddhism was another religion important to the Chinese. From around the time of the T'ang dynasty (A.D. 618–907), Buddhists built temples along the riverbanks and carved statues of the Buddha on cliffs overlooking the river.

In A.D. 713, a Buddhist monk began building this statue of the Buddha, hoping it would protect boats passing on the rough river waters below. The statue was cut into cliffs beside the Min River, a tributary of the Yangtze in Sichuan.

Taming the Waters

For centuries, the Chinese have tried to control the waters of the Yangtze and its tributaries. All Chinese children learn about Yu the Great, who is said to have been the founder of China's first dynasty about 4,000 years ago. According to legend, Yu worked for thirteen years without stopping. He built dikes and channels to control flooding on the Yangtze River, and he never once returned home to see his wife and children.

> **❝ It was a moving sight...
> to see more than three hundred
> human beings reduced to the
> level of work animals. ❞**
> John Hersey, describing men
> hauling boats through the Three
> Gorges in *A Single Pebble* (1914)

Bringing tea down the Yangtze River could be very hazardous. Many boats sank on the most dangerous stretch of rapids in the Three Gorges. Records show that in 1899 alone, more than fifty boats were wrecked along the river.

Evidence exists that the people of the Yangtze basin created networks of irrigation channels and ditches to grow rice thousands of years ago. In the Sichuan basin, an irrigation system that dates back over 2,000 years is still used today. Over the centuries, the Chinese built ditches and dikes to protect the surrounding land from flooding.

Navigating the Three Gorges

Until the late twentieth century, **navigating** on the Three Gorges was a major undertaking. Traveling upstream through the gorges, against the powerful currents, was especially difficult. Boats had to be pulled from the shore by teams of 100 to 300 men hauling long ropes. On the steep-sided sections of the river, steps and paths were cut into the cliffs. Teams of men clung on ropes as they strained to drag the boats upriver. In the early twentieth century, a boat trip from Yichang to Chongqing could take forty to fifty days, but the same trip downriver, from Chongqing to Yichang, usually took only five to twelve days.

By the mid-twentieth century, the channel through the Three Gorges had been made much safer. Today, modern boats have powerful engines that allow them to fight the strong currents in the gorges.

Chapter 3
CITIES AND SETTLEMENTS

A Huge Population

China has about 1.3 billion people — the largest population of any country in the world. On a map, the country seems to have plenty of space, but most of the land in the west and north is covered with mountains or deserts. A relatively small area of land — roughly one-tenth of China's total area — is suitable for people to live.

Around one-third of all China's people live in the Yangtze basin, which is almost three times the size of Texas. The population of the Yangtze basin is more than the combined populations of the United States and Canada.

This map shows the main cities and towns in the Yangtze basin.

MONGOLIA

N

Beijing

NORTH KOREA

SOUTH KOREA

Yellow Sea

0   500   1000 km

0   500 miles

Grand Canal

Lanzhou

Zhengzhou

Nanjing

Shanghai

Xi'an

Ma'anshan

Hangzhou

C H I N A

East China Sea

Yangtze (Jinsha)

Wuhan

TIBETAN PLATEAU

Chengdu

Yichang

Three Gorges

Poyang Lake

Dongting Lake

Yangtze (Chang)

Chongqing

Yuan

Xiang

Gan

Lhasa

Yibin

TAIWAN

BHUTAN

Zhangzhou

INDIA

MYANMAR (BURMA)

Guangzhou

South China Sea

Tropic of Cancer

VIETNAM

18

A porter carries a load of soil from a boat to the shore at Chongqing. The city is built on hills above the river, so everything has to be taken up steps from the boats to the city center.

Chongqing

The city of Chongqing, which dates back some 2,500 years, has been a busy port and trading center for centuries. Today, it is one of the largest urban areas in the world. The city is located at the meeting point of the Jialing and the Yangtze Rivers. The old part of the city is sandwiched between the two rivers. Dusty, gray apartment buildings and shining new office towers cling to the steep slopes that rise from the water, and bridges and cable cars span the two rivers.

The port of Chongqing is the furthest point that large boats can travel up the Yangtze, and the city's riverbanks are lined with barges. Thousands of porters (called the *bang bang jun*, or "helpful army") stagger under heavy loads that hang from poles over their shoulders. The porters carry supplies up and down steep steps that lead to the river. A new harbor is now being constructed for larger ships.

In addition to being an important port, Chongqing is also a major industrial center. The city is heavily polluted, and a thick **smog** hangs over it, especially in the damp winters. Its homes and factories sprawl for miles in every direction, while new housing and industries are spreading into the countryside around it.

POPULATIONS OF CITIES ALONG THE YANGTZE

- Chongqing: 30,000,000
- Shanghai: 15,600,000
- Wuhan: 4,000,000
- Nanjing: 1,800,000
- Yichang: 500,000

Nanjing Road in Shanghai is China's busiest shopping district. Shanghai is so crowded that different groups of workers take different days off to make getting around easier.

Shanghai

Shanghai is the center for China's trade and industry. It has the largest port in China and is also the country's most fashionable city. The city lies beside the Huangpu River, a tributary at the mouth of the Yangtze. The name Shanghai means "on the sea."

Shanghai developed as a port and industrial city during the 1800s, when foreigners used it as their main trading base in China. It was famous as a city of adventure and pleasure and was one of the leading trading centers in east Asia.

In the 1990s, a massive new building program began in Shanghai, and the city's skyline is now filled with skyscrapers. A new area called Pudong has been developed on what was once farmland and slums. Pudong has offices, shops, and industrial areas linked to central Shanghai by subway, bridges, and tunnels.

In addition to the construction of new buildings in the city of Shanghai, ten new settlements have recently been built in the Yangtze delta. These settlements are intended to provide homes for over a million people in the crowded delta.

Nanjing

Nanjing means "southern capital." The city is still partially surrounded by the huge walls that were built to protect it when it was the capital of China during the Ming dynasty. Towers, temples, and palaces, some rebuilt and some in ruins, still remain among the new buildings and busy roads. Nanjing's wide streets are lined with trees that provide

> **Great changes are afoot: A bridge will fly to span the north and south.**
>
> Mao Zedong, writing about the first bridge to be built across the Yangtze, in the poem *Swimming* (1956)

This long bridge was the first to be built across the Yangtze River. A double-decker, it carries both trains and road vehicles. Before it was built, all traffic, including trains, that traveled north and south in China had to be taken across the river by ferry.

shade from the intense summer heat, and the city has parks, gardens, and lakes. Nanjing is also a large port and a wealthy industrial city that benefits from being close to Shanghai.

Wuhan

At Wuhan, the Yangtze is joined by the Han River, its longest tributary. Oceangoing ships can sail up the Yangtze as far as Wuhan, and during the 1800s, it was the main port in China for the tea trade. In the 1920s, Wuhan was linked to Beijing by railroads and became the first major industrial city in central China. The first bridge across the Yangtze River was built in Wuhan in 1957. The bridge was named the "Iron and Steel Rainbow" by Mao Zedong. Since then, Wuhan has grown into a large industrial city.

Villages and Farms

Every scrap of land in the lower Yangtze valley is farmed. The landscape is dotted with small villages and groups of houses that are owned and run by families or village units. Villages in low-lying areas have ponds, which are often stocked with fish, and many have a shady grove of bamboo trees. The larger villages have a school, and the towns hold markets once a week.

Village homes are usually single-story structures made of wood or mud brick with dirt, stone, or concrete floors. (Wealthy farmers might build two-story brick houses.) The homes have a living room, storeroom, and one or two bedrooms, with a few simple pieces of bamboo furniture. Most homes have electricity. Some have television, but few have refrigerators or washing machines.

These Tibetan children live in tents on the Tibetan Plateau. Their families herd animals on horseback. Children in this region learn to ride horses soon after they learn to walk.

On the edge of the Tibetan Plateau, where the Yangtze River has its source, a Tibetan village is built on a patch of flat land with steep slopes all around. No roads lead to this village, just rough paths and tracks. The villagers grow barley in their fields.

In villages, running water piped to homes is still a luxury, and families usually get their water from the river or from a shared tap or well.

Mountain Homes

Relatively few people live on the high plateau near the source of the Yangtze, where the harsh climate and poor soil make farming difficult. Those who do live there are mostly Tibetan. Living in small villages, they grow barley and vegetables. Many keep yaks or sheep that roam the plateau grazing on sparse grass. Their homes are made of mud brick or sometimes wood, with dirt floors. They may have a small cooking stove that uses wood or yak dung for fuel. Some Tibetan people are nomads, moving from place to place as the seasons change. They erect cloth tents when they find a good grazing area for their animals.

In the mountains and valleys where the Yangtze flows down from the plateau, other tribes of non-Chinese people, such as the Yi and the Naxi, can be found. The ancestors of these people were forced into the mountains as the Chinese settled in the valleys of the Yangtze. They have dug terraces, or steps, along the sides of the steep hillsides so they can grow what they need to eat, and they keep a few animals such as chickens and pigs. Their villages are small groups of simple wooden houses, which are often perched high on the side of a valley. These mountainous areas have few schools and no stores, and a walk to the closest town can take many hours.

> **❝ I get by growing oranges and peanuts. My family have been here for generations, but now the young people think working the land is too hard. They leave to find work in the towns. ❞**
> Wang Zuolu, a farmer in the Three Gorges area.

23

Chapter 4

ECONOMIC ACTIVITY

ECONOMIC ACTIVITY

> **❝ *Even a clever daughter-in-law cannot cook a meal without rice.* ❞**
> Traditional Chinese proverb

Land of Fish and Rice

The lower Yangtze valley, from the Three Gorges to the ocean, is the most important farming region in China. Its warm, wet climate is ideal for growing rice, and about 70 percent of China's rice is grown there. Wheat is grown in the valley during the winter. The valley's hundreds of rivers, lakes, and ponds are all teeming with fish. Roughly half of the freshwater fish in China comes from this region, which is especially famous for its carp and shellfish, such as shrimp and crabs. The lower Yangtze valley is sometimes called the land of fish and rice.

A farmer fertilizes her crop of rice by hand. North of the Yangtze River, where the winter is too cold and dry for growing rice, wheat is the main crop. South of the Yangtze River, conditions are perfect for growing rice.

Farming Silk

Silk is an ancient Chinese material that is still produced by farmers in the lower Yangtze valley. Silk worms are the caterpillars of the silk moth. Kept indoors on large bamboo trays, the caterpillars are fed chopped leaves from mulberry trees until they spin cocoons of fine silk thread. Each cocoon can contain as much as a half mile of thread. Farmers take the cocoons to factories, where the thread is unraveled and spun into silk.

Rice Facts

- Rice is believed to have been grown in the Yangtze delta as early as 5000 B.C.
- In order to grow, rice needs a warm, wet climate. It is grown in paddy fields, which are filled with water.
- In hilly areas, such as those found in the Sichuan basin, the land is terraced (made into steps) so that rice can be grown on the slopes.

Other Crops

Many farmers in the lower Yangtze valley grow fuit and cotton, and this area produces about half the cotton grown in China. Tea is also grown on slopes in sheltered areas. Almost every Chinese farmer grows vegetables. Some vegetables are kept for a farmer's own use, and some are sold in markets to feed people in the cities.

Fish is an important food in the Yangtze basin. This fisherman is using cormorants, which dive into the water and catch fish. String is tied around the birds' throats so they cannot swallow. When the birds come back to the boat, the fisherman takes the fish out of their mouths.

Using the Land

The Chinese have always made the most of their land — very little is wasted. Two or three different crops are often grown side by side. Waste food is fed to animals such as pigs, and human waste is often used to fertilize the fields. Little space exists for grazing animals, but pigs, chickens, and ducks are kept for their meat and eggs. Many farmers cannot afford modern machinery, so heavy work, such as plowing, is often done using water buffalo. Rice is planted and harvested by hand.

A Transportation Route

Until the mid-twentieth century, when railroads began to be the main form of transportation in China, the Yangtze River was an extremely busy waterway. Few roads existed in China, and overland travel meant passing through mountains filled with bandits. The Yangtze River was a bit like China's main street. Traveling upriver, however, was not always easy. During winter, low water levels and shifting sandbars could cause ships to run aground. Navigation in the Three Gorges was especially difficult and dangerous.

This boat is a sampan, a traditional Chinese river craft. Some families live on their boats and spend their lives traveling along the river.

River Craft

The traditional small riverboat on the Yangtze is the sampan, which means "three planks." In the past, many Chinese lived on their boats, and some still do today. Goods were once carried by large wooden sailboats, called junks, but barges with engines now carry heavy cargo. Foreigners brought steamboats to China in the mid-1800s. For a while, Americans sailing the Yangtze used paddle wheelers, such as those found on the Mississippi River. Today, fast **hydrofoil** boats speed between the larger cities.

A Safe Channel

Over the last hundred years, the Yangtze has been made much safer for ships. The river has been **dredged**, and rocks in the Three Gorges have been removed with explosives. Railroads now carry a large amount of freight, but about 70 percent of China's shipping is still done on the Yangtze. Barges are used to bring coal and concrete up the river, often traveling in long convoys linked to a single tugboat. Many small fishing boats can be found on the Yangtze, and hundreds of ferries link the towns on its banks.

> **"** *The Grand Canal is like a man's throat: if it does not supply grain for a day, Beijing would die.* **"**
> Chinese government official, writing in 1421

The Grand Canal

Crops grown in the Yangtze basin have always been important to the Chinese, and they have built canals to ship the region's food to other parts of China. The most spectacular of these canals is the Grand Canal. Stretching from Hangzhou to Beijing in northern China, it is over 1,100 miles (1,770 km) long. Some sections were started in the fifth century B.C., but the main canal was dug in the sixth and seventh centuries A.D. Today, much of the canal is ruined, but about 700 miles (1,126 km) of it is still in use. The Chinese are planning to use the canal in the future to carry water from the Yangtze River to parts of northern China, where water shortages exist.

A boat carries coal through Wu Gorge in the Three Gorges section of the Yangtze. The river provides a cheap and easy way to transport heavy, bulky goods.

Industrial Development

Workers weld pipes at the Three Gorges Dam. When the dam is finished, it will provide hydroelectric power to millions of factories along the Yangtze.

Until the mid-twentieth century, most people in China were farmers. When the communists took over the country in 1949, however, they began building factories for the production of iron and steel, which were used to make trains, railroads, and machinery. To provide fuel for factories, hundreds of coal mines were opened. The communists also encouraged smaller factories in towns across China to make basic products, such as bricks, farming machinery, and tools. They built railroads and roads to move goods around the country. In 1970, work began on the Gezhouba Dam, which crosses the Yangtze River at the lower end of the Three Gorges. Completed in 1986, the dam supplies electricity to factories in the Yangtze River valley.

Mining and Industry

China, which is the largest coal producer in the world, is rich in **minerals**. Both coal and iron ore are mined at several sites along the Yangtze valley. Close to Nanjing is the huge mining town of Ma'anshan. The iron mined here supplies steelworks in Ma'anshan and Shanghai. Further upstream, in Wuhan, one of China's largest steelworks employs over 120,000 people.

Many towns along the Yangtze River have chemical factories that make fertilizers for farmers. They also have many engineering firms making machinery and factories producing construction materials. In addition to such factories, Shanghai has shipbuilding industries around its great port.

Paper, Textiles, and Food

Paper mills are found all along the Yangtze, having been built beside the river because papermaking needs huge amounts of water. Paper was first made in China. The spinning and weaving of silk is another ancient industry in China. Silk is still woven in Nanjing, but textiles made from cotton and manmade fabrics are now more important to the Chinese economy. Many towns along the Yangtze River have food processing factories, including the town of Zhenjian, which is famous for its vinegar and pickled vegetables.

New Industries

Improved living standards in China have led to a huge growth in factories that make consumer goods, such as televisions and refrigerators. Shanghai is one of China's leading producers of electrical and high-technology goods.

Logs are brought down the Yangtze by ship to be used in factories. Timber is also used for building and papermaking, but because wood is scarce in the lower Yangtze valley, paper mills often use wheat, rice straw, and other plant fibers from the surrounding countryside.

> **The river is the factory's blood. We pump millions of gallons a day out of it to make paper.**
> Jia Zhijie, manager of a paper mill on the Yangtze

Chapter 5

ANIMALS AND PLANTS

Giant Pandas

The giant panda is the national symbol of China. Western China is the only place in the world where it is found.

The most famous animal of the Yangtze basin is the giant panda — known as the "big bear-cat" in Chinese. Giant pandas only live in China. They were once found in forests all across the southern region of the country. Today, however, little forest is left in the Yangtze basin, except in remote mountain areas, and pandas only survive in parts of the western Sichuan basin. Even there, they are not safe, because forests are still being cut down for timber, and poachers hunt pandas for their fur. Pandas are now an endangered species. No one knows exactly how many still survive, but there are thought to be between 400 and 1,000 left in the wild.

In 1980, with the help of the World Wildlife Fund (WWF), the Chinese government created a special panda reserve called Wolong in the Sichuan basin. At Wolong, a breeding program has been established to save the giant panda from becoming extinct. Many of the pandas in the reserve have radio-controlled monitoring devices attached to them to track their movements. Anyone caught harming a panda is arrested.

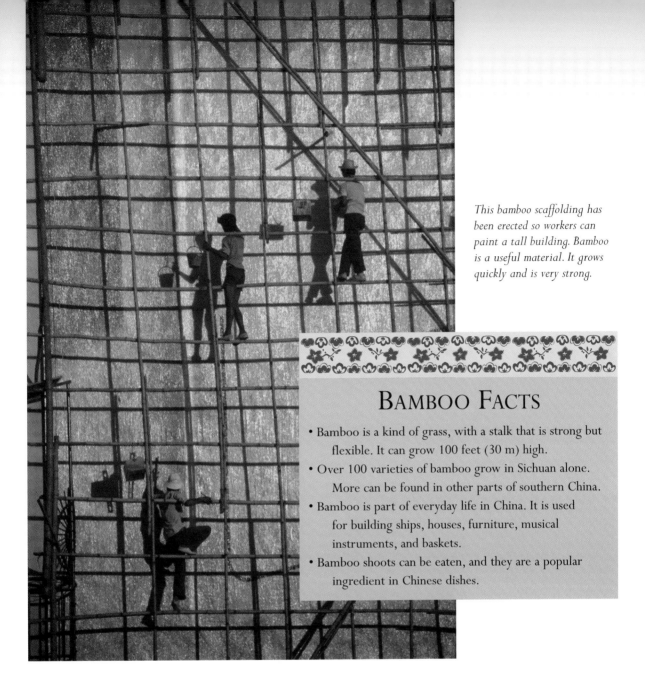

This bamboo scaffolding has been erected so workers can paint a tall building. Bamboo is a useful material. It grows quickly and is very strong.

BAMBOO FACTS

- Bamboo is a kind of grass, with a stalk that is strong but flexible. It can grow 100 feet (30 m) high.
- Over 100 varieties of bamboo grow in Sichuan alone. More can be found in other parts of southern China.
- Bamboo is part of everyday life in China. It is used for building ships, houses, furniture, musical instruments, and baskets.
- Bamboo shoots can be eaten, and they are a popular ingredient in Chinese dishes.

Bamboo Plants

Pandas are mainly **herbivorous** and feed on the stems or leaves of bamboo plants. They eat a huge amount of bamboo every day and prefer a particular kind called fountain bamboo. Bamboo flowers at extremely long intervals that are sometimes as much as a hundred years apart, and after it has flowered, it dies. In 1980, large areas of fountain bamboo all flowered at the same time and then died. Many pandas starved to death.

31

Snow leopards have been hunted almost to extinction for their beautiful fur. Today, only about 200 to 300 snow leopards are left in the wild. Kept warm by their thick coats, the leopards live high in the mountains of western China.

Mountain Wildlife

Near the source of the Yangtze, on the Tibetan Plateau, the climate is extremely cold and usually very dry. Only a few trees, grasses, and low shrubs are able to grow there. Small rodents, such as pikas and marmots (small rabbitlike creatures), scurry among the rocks. Larger animals, such as deer, sheep, and yaks, graze on the sparse grass. Eagles and snow leopards prey on the smaller animals.

Upper Yangtze

In the valleys and hills of the upper Yangtze, there is more shelter and food so wildlife is more varied. Several species of monkey live among the trees, including the golden monkey with its long, thick, golden fur and light-blue face. Another brightly-colored creature is the golden pheasant, which has gold and red feathers and long tail feathers. Like many creatures along the Yangtze, these animals are endangered.

Many plants that grow along the upper Yangtze, such as rhododendrons, azaleas, peonies, and camellias, are now grown in gardens all over the world. Herbs and fungi found in the foothills of the mountains are used by the Chinese in medicines.

> ***It will be a long job educating the Chinese to love birds.***
> Tang Xiyang, editor of the Chinese magazine *Nature*, quoted in *Tears of the Dragon* (1992)

Lower Yangtze

The Chinese dolphin, which is found only in the waters of the lower Yangtze, is one of the rarest animals in China. Less than twenty Chinese dolphins are believed to be left in the world. The Chinese alligator is also very rare, and both the dolphin and the alligator are now protected from hunters by law.

The marshy Poyang Lake provides a winter home to many birds that migrate from further north. Almost the entire world population of Siberian cranes spends the winter on Poyang Lake. In the summer, the water in the lake rises and floods the surrounding land, creating sheltered, shallow-water breeding grounds for fish.

Disappearing Wildlife

Much of the Yangtze valley has been stripped of its wildlife, especially along the river's lower course. Very little land in the region is not used by people, and natural **habitats** have been damaged by pollution. Wild animals such as snakes and monkeys are often hunted for food, and some are killed for their skins. Birds are also threatened because people kill them for food and to use their feathers as ornaments. To protect the creatures that are left, several nature reserves have been created in the Yangtze valley.

Golden monkeys make their home in high mountain forests in the upper Yangtze valley, where they eat wild fruits and tender leaves. Much of the forests have been cut down, and golden monkeys are now very rare.

33

Chapter 6

ENVIRONMENTAL ISSUES

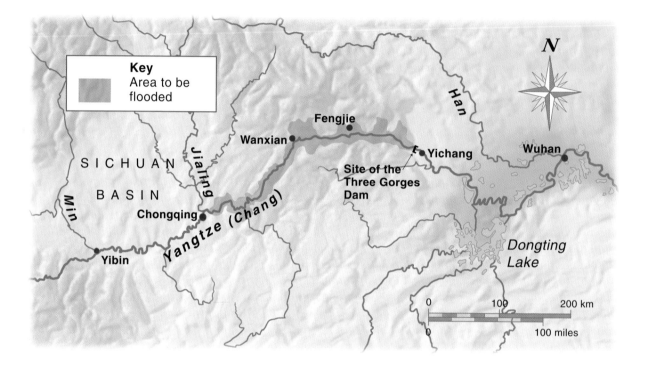

Key
Area to be flooded

SICHUAN BASIN

Min

Jialing

Yangtze (Chang)

Yibin

Chongqing

Wanxian

Fengjie

Site of the Three Gorges Dam

Yichang

Han

Wuhan

Dongting Lake

N

0   100   200 km

0   100 miles

This map shows the site of the Three Gorges Dam and the region the new reservoir will cover.

The Three Gorges Dam

Just downstream from the Three Gorges, a huge dam is being built across the Yangtze River. It is the largest construction project to be carried out in China since the building of the Great Wall of China more than 2,000 years ago. When the dam is finished, it will be the largest and most powerful dam in the world.

Behind the dam, the waters of the Yangtze River will gradually rise, creating a vast **reservoir** that will stretch through the Three Gorges and as far upstream as Chongqing. In some places, the water level will rise as much as 360 feet (110 m). Farmland, towns, and villages will be covered by water.

> **When the dam is built, the opportunities here will be limitless!**
> Zhang Mingtai, factory manager in Wanxian

Hydroelectric Power

One of the main reasons for building the dam is to generate electricity for the 400 million people who live in the Yangtze valley. Many cities and industrial sites in central China suffer from shortages of electricity. Twenty-six generators on the dam will produce enough electricity to serve cities as far away as Shanghai.

Other Benefits

The dam is also supposed to control the flow of water in the Yangtze, reducing flooding beyond the dam. In addition, the reservoir behind the dam will cause the water level in the river to rise, so large ships weighing up to 10,000 tons (9,000 metric tons) will be able to travel as far west as Chongqing. The Chinese hope less-developed inland regions of China, especially the Sichuan basin, will benefit, because an improved waterway and a plentiful supply of inexpensive electricity should attract new industries.

Construction work has begun on the Three Gorges Dam, one of the largest dam projects ever undertaken in the world. The dam is supposed to supply huge amounts of non-polluting electricity and control the river to reduce flooding.

THE THREE GORGES PROJECT

- The dam will be 1.25 miles (2 km) long and approximately 600 feet (183 m) high.
- The reservoir behind the dam will stretch as far as Chongqing. It will measure almost 400 miles (643km) long — about the length of Lake Superior.
- People in 1,400 towns and villages will be resettled in new homes.
- The dam, which was begun in 1993, should be finished by 2009, taking sixteen years to build.
- The costs of the project keep rising, and it may end up costing about $30 billion.

Problems of the Dam

Many Chinese are concerned about the effects of the new dam. Thousands of homes, factories, and farms will be destroyed as the huge reservoir created by the dam fills. In total, about 1.2 million people are being moved so the dam can be built. Although they will be provided new places to live, many find it heartbreaking to leave their old homes. Farmers complain that the new land they are being given is higher in the hills and not as fertile as the land in the valley.

In addition, the dam's massive proportions present dangers. If, for example, an earthquake caused the dam to collapse, millions of people living downstream would be swept away. Some people believe the Yangtze River's waters will slow down upon entering the reservoir and will deposit large amounts of sediment. This sediment might eventually clog the reservoir, making it impossible for large ships to pass through and blocking the dam's electricity generators.

This bridge lies above the city of Fengjie in the Three Gorges area. Water in the reservoir behind the Three Gorges Dam will eventually reach as high as the bridge. All the buildings below it will be covered in water. About 65,000 people in the area are being moved to a new location.

Changing Landscape

The reservoir will forever change the natural splendor of the Three Gorges, a region with deep ties to China's artistic and spiritual past. Soon, the waters of the Yangtze River will no longer surge through steep-sided gorges. Instead, the region will contain a calm lake. Hundreds of ancient tombs and temples, many of which have never been studied closely, will be covered by water, and China will lose one of its greatest tourist sights.

Wildlife in Danger

The dam will also have consequences for wildlife in the Yangtze River and its valley. Fish will not be able to swim upriver to lay their eggs, and changes in the flow of sediment may leave fish and other water creatures with shortages of their natural food. Many people fear the reservoir will become a polluted soup of chemicals and sewage that have traveled down the river from Chongqing.

> **" *I couldn't bear it. I was crying in my heart.* "**
> Zhu Guobing, a farmer moved from his home in the Three Gorges to make way for the new reservoir

A Different Plan

Critics of the Three Gorges Dam claim that a series of smaller dams on the tributaries of the Yangtze River would be safer and more effective than one large dam. They also argue that flooding downstream could be better controlled by creating overflow lakes, which could store floodwater.

VANISHING WANXIAN

Wanxian is a city located beside the Yangtze in the Three Gorges section of the river. Once the reservoir created by the new dam fills, two-thirds of the city will be covered by water. Nine hundred factories lie in the path of the rising water, and these factories will have to be moved. In addition, a new city is being built higher in the mountains for the 800,000 people who are being moved from the Wanxian area.

37

Trees are cut down far upstream, tied together in rafts of logs, and floated down the Yangtze. When the trees are cut down, rain often washes the soil away. Some 500 million tons (450 million m tons) of soil end up in the Yangtze every year — as much as in the Nile, Amazon, and Mississippi Rivers put together.

Pollution

Every city in the Yangtze valley is choking with high levels of air pollution. A thick smog, for example, hangs over the city of Chongqing, and in 1990 the city spent thousands of dollars to replace buses and lampposts that had been eaten away by **acid rain**. Acid rain is also causing forests in Sichuan to die. Part of the problem is the use of coal as a main energy source. About three-quarters of China's power is supplied by burning coal, which produces harmful gases and dust. China already uses more coal than any other country in the world. If China becomes a big energy consumer like the United States (where people use ten times as much energy per head as in China), the effects could be disastrous.

The Yangtze River has become a sewer running through central China. The Chinese rely on huge amounts of artificial fertilizers for their crops, and the chemicals run off into the river. Industrial waste and sewage from the millions of homes along the valley is dumped into the Yangtze. Each year, over 1 billion tons (.9 billion m tons) of waste pour into the Yangtze River.

Losing Forests

The Chinese keep pushing further into remote areas to cut down trees. They clear the trees to create more farmland and use the timber for fuel and building houses. Since the 1950s, more than a third of Sichuan's forests have been cleared. Once the trees are cut down, rain washes away the soil and the land becomes useless for farming.

Soil that is washed away by the rain pours into the rivers, and it is then carried along as sediment and dropped further downstream. The sediment narrows the river channels and fills up lakes on the plains of the lower Yangtze valley. Lakes such as Dongting and Poyang Lakes are shrinking in size and cannot contain as much floodwater as they did in the past. The severe floods of the 1980s and 1990s were mainly due to increased sediment levels in the lower Yangtze River and its lakes.

China has enacted laws to prevent factories from polluting rivers, but most factory owners do not follow these laws. The government encourages tree planting on hillsides and tries to limit the number of trees that are cut down. Controlling what people do in the remote mountain areas of China, however, is not easy.

> **" The smog is sometimes so thick you can flavor your food with it! "**
> Hu Hongrong, river worker in Chongqing

Along the Yangtze, smoke pours out of factories in all major cities and towns, which have high levels of air pollution.

Chapter 7

LEISURE AND RECREATION

Tourism on the River

The Yangtze is a working river and is not used much for leisure, except in the Three Gorges area. Many Chinese people, particularly in the countryside, do not have the time or money to take a vacation.

More Chinese are now traveling around China, however, and they enjoy visiting their country's famous sights. The Three Gorges is one of the most popular places to visit. Cruise boats crammed with people leave Chongqing and sail down the Yangtze. Most boats stop at historical sites and temples along the way. This tourist activity will most likely change, however, when the reservoir behind the new dam fills. Some people believe tourists will no longer come to the area, but others say the new reservoir will become a tourist attraction itself.

Temples and Mountains

The Chinese also visit historic towns along the Yangtze. These ancient towns and cities, such as Nanjing, Hangzhou, and Yangzhou (at the junction of the Grand Canal and the Yangtze) have beautiful temples, gardens, and lakes, many of which date back hundreds of years.

Lushan is a beautiful mountain overlooking Poyang Lake that the Chinese like to visit to escape the summer heat. Narrow mountain paths wind past waterfalls, and visitors sip the special Misty Cloud green tea. Other scenic spots in the mountains bordering the Yangtze are Huang Shan and Emei Shan, two sacred mountains with towering rocks, bamboo groves, and temples.

> **"** *Who needs to go to the theater with the entertainment available in Chinese families? Someone will be sure to be a musician of some kind. Another cousin can do remarkable gymnastic tricks on his bicycle, and we can waste a whole afternoon watching him perform.* **"**
> Mr. Li from Hong Kong, describing a visit to relatives in Shanghai

Fun Away from Home

Houses and apartments in China's cities and towns have little space. When Chinese people are not watching television, they like to spend their spare time outside their homes. Many people visit parks, where they take walks, fly kites, or enjoy boating on ponds. Sichuan is famous for its teahouses, where people go to visit and play card games, **mah-jongg**, or Chinese chess. During a long, hot summer along the Yangtze River, the Chinese enjoy eating popsicles and slices of watermelon. They sit outside their houses until late in the evening, fanning themselves to keep cool.

Clouds swirl through the steep slopes of the sacred mountain Huang Shan. Its landscape is often painted by Chinese artists. Millions of Chinese tourists come every year to climb the mountain and gaze at the scenery.

Time to Relax

The Chinese enjoy shopping in big cities such as Shanghai. Streams
of people wander in and out of stores and gaze in the windows at
the new fashions. Small towns have weekly markets, and farming
families pour into the towns from the countryside, mixing business
with pleasure. Every town has street stalls where people can sit
down for a snack. In the cities, many people eat out at restaurants,
and in the evenings, young people visit bars, where they listen to
or sing karaoke.

In parks and open spaces all along the Yangtze, people exercise
in the early morning. Some people like to practise tai chi, a gentle
martial art that uses controlled breathing and movements, while
others exercise to music by dancing or doing aerobics. Young people
enjoy sports such as basketball and volleyball. In many areas of the
countryside around the Yangtze River, children swim in streams in
the heat of the summer.

DRAGON BOAT FESTIVAL

The Dragon Boat festival is held in memory of a poet named Qu Yuan. About 300 B.C., he drowned himself in a river near the Yangtze. Rowers race each other in decorated boats that often have dragonheads on the bow. Crowds cheer, let off fireworks, and beat drums to encourage the rowers to go faster. Visitors to the festival often eat *zongzi*, a kind of sticky rice wrapped in bamboo leaves.

Festivals

The Chinese celebrate several festivals during the year, the largest of which is the Chinese New Year, held in January or February. Before the New Year, people clean out their houses and put up red decorations (red is a lucky color in China). Trains, buses, and ferries are jammed with people returning home to be with their families. At home, feasts are prepared and everyone stays up late to see in the New Year. Processions with lion and dragon dancers snake through the streets, and millions of firecrackers and fireworks are set off all over the country.

The Sun rises over the Pudong district of Shanghai. In a quiet time before the busy city awakens, a man practises tai chi.

Chapter 8

THE FUTURE

THE FUTURE

Crowds of city dwellers stroll down Nanjing Road in Shanghai. The Yangtze basin has some of the wealthiest regions in China, where many people have good jobs and a high standard of living.

Rapid Development

China has one of the fastest-growing economies in the world. Compared to fifty years ago, Chinese people are wealthier and better educated and their lives are much easier. The Yangtze basin is at the heart of these changes and is set to grow as fast as, if not faster than, any other region in China. Although not China's capital, Shanghai is the most important city in the country with its new industries and trendsetting people. Inland, cities such as Chongqing will grow enormously because of the Three Gorges Dam project.

Development in the Yangtze basin, however, is uneven. While lifestyles in the big cities are becoming more like those in the United States, many areas in the countryside remain relatively backward. People from poorer rural areas are pouring into the cities, looking for work and riches. Some succeed, but many end up on the streets. Unemployment is becoming worse because many of the old state-run industries are now laying off their employees.

Taking Care of Millions

In the second half of the twentieth century, better living standards and medical care and increased amounts of food and clean water led to swift population growth in China. In 1979, China's government decided to limit families to only one child. The measure was intended to help control the population explosion, but the number of people in China is still growing. More than one-third of the country's people live in the Yangtze basin. They all need homes and jobs, and they also want fashionable clothes and new household goods. This growing population will require more land, electricity, and water.

> *There is only one Yangtze River, and we have already subjected it to many stupid deeds.* **"**
> Chinese journalist Dai Qing, writing in *Yangtze! Yangtze!: Debate over the Three Gorges Project* (1994)

The Future of the River

The Yangtze River is a lifeline for the millions of people living along its banks. Besides providing a major transportation route and a supply of water, it provides electricity to homes and industries. Environmental problems, however, are mounting. Today, most Chinese believe the benefits of rapid economic growth outweigh its costs, such as pollution to the environment. Whether the Chinese can increase their standard of living without damaging the Yangtze River forever is a big question for the future.

In a village along the upper reaches of the Yangtze, a farmer carries a load of twigs to her house. Many places along the river have changed little in hundreds of years.

GLOSSARY

acid rain: rain containing harmful chemicals from car exhaust and other sources.

basin: the area of land drained by a river and its tributaries.

Bhuddist: relating to Bhuddism, a religion founded in India in the fifth century B.C. by Siddhartha Gautama, or "Buddha."

communism: a political system in which the government controls the economy and owns most or all property.

delta: a flat, triangular area of land where a river empties into a large body of water, such as an ocean, through many channels.

dikes: barriers built along a riverbank to prevent flooding.

dredge: to clear mud, sand, or rock from a river or bay so boats can travel more easily.

dynasty: a succession of rulers belonging to the same family.

gorges: valleys with extremely steep sides.

habitats: places where a particular plant or animal usually lives and grows.

herbivorous: eats plants.

hydroelectric: creates electricity through the power of rushing water.

hydrofoil: a kind of boat that rises partially out of the water and skims along the surface.

irrigation: the process of bringing water to fields using channels or pipes.

mah-jongg: a Chinese game that involves tiles of different designs.

meanders: takes a winding course.

Middle Ages: a period of European history between about A.D. 500 and 1500.

mineral: substances found in the earth, such as iron ore, that are not plant or animal material and are obtained by mining.

monsoon: a strong, seasonal wind that blows over the Indian ocean and southern Asia and brings heavy rains.

navigating: guiding a boat on a safe course.

plateau: an area of flat land that rises above the surrounding land.

reservoir: a natural or artificial pond or lake that is used for storing water.

sediment: small pieces of soil and rock that are carried and deposited by a river.

smog: the mixture of fog and pollution.

source: the point of origin for the waters of a river or stream.

Taoists: followers of Taoism, a Chinese philosophy and religion dating back to about the fourth century B.C.

tributaries: small streams or rivers that feed into larger rivers.

tung oil: an oil made from the seeds of the tung tree that is mainly used in varnish for waterproofing wood.

FURTHER INFORMATION

TIME LINE

B.C.

c. 2000	According to Chinese legend, Yu the Great organizes flood control on the Yangtze River.
475–256	Kingdom of Chou controls much of the middle Yangtze River area.
250	A huge project to control the waters of the Min River in the Sichuan basin is organized.
221	Ch'in emperor unites China's kingdoms.

A.D.

610	Main section of the Grand Canal is built.
618–906	T'ang dynasty rules China, and temples are built in many locations along the Yangtze.
1127	Sung dynasty establishes its capital in Hangzhou.
1368	Ming dynasty establishes its capital in Nanjing.
1840	The first steamboats are used on the Yangtze River.
1938	Chongqing becomes the Chinese capital while eastern China is occupied by the Japanese.
1949	Communists take control of China.
1986	The Gezhouba Dam is completed.
1993	Construction of the Three Gorges Dam begins.

BOOKS

Cotterell, Arthur. *Ancient China* (Knopf, 2000)

Goh, Sui Noi. *China* (Gareth Stevens, 1998)

Green, Robert. *China* (Lucent Books, 1999)

Lewis, Elizabeth Foreman. *Young Fu of the Upper Yangtze* (Holt Rinehart and Winston, 2000)

Martin, Patricia A. Fink. *Giant Pandas* (Children's Press, 2002)

Pollard, Michael. *The Yangtze* (Benchmark Books, 1998)

WEB SITES

Digital Photo Gallery: Yangtze River
www.asahi-net.or.jp/~cu4w-kwsm/ chin960/fwb806.htm
Numerous photographs of the Yangtze and the river's surrounding regions.

Great Wall Across the Yangtze
www.pbs.org/itus/greatwall/
An in-depth look at the Three Gorges Dam Project.

The Water Page: Yangtze River
www.thewaterpage.com/yangtze.htm
Many facts about the river, with information about the Three Gorges Dam.

Yangtze River
http://hrl.harvard.edu/~zhchen/ topic/yangtze/yangtze.html
Information about the Yangtze, with photographs of the Three Gorges section of the river.

The Yangtze River
www.ces10.k12.wi.us/Ecosystems/ water/Yangtze
A site about the Yangtze River created by six-graders.

Yu Yuan: The Garden of Peace and Comfort
www.yuyuangarden.com
Panoramic shots of Yu Yuan, a famous garden in the center of Shanghai that is more than 400 years old.

47

INDEX
INDEX

Numbers in **boldface** type refer to illustrations and maps.